PENGUINS!

BY GAIL GIBBONS

HOLIDAY HOUSE/NEW YORK

For Jeffrey and Ken Goldfarb

Special thanks to
Jennifer Guille and Dyan deNapoli
of the New England Aquarium,
Boston, Massachusetts

Library of Congress Cataloging-in-Publication Data
Gibbons, Gail.
    Penguins! / by Gail Gibbons. — 1st ed.
        p.   cm.
    Summary: Describes the habitat, physical characteristics, and
behavior of different kinds of penguins.
    ISBN 0-8234-1388-8
    1. Penguins—Juvenile literature.   [1. Penguins.]   I. Title.
QL696.S473G44   1998   98-5194   CIP   AC
598.47—dc21
    ISBN 0-8234-1516-3 (pbk.)

Here come the penguins, straight and tall. They walk with a waddle, yet look stately and dignified.

SOME KINDS OF PENGUINS

EMPEROR PENGUIN

KING PENGUIN

CHINSTRAP PENGUIN

MACARONI PENGUIN

LITTLE BLUE PENGUIN also called FAIRY PENGUIN

GENTOO PENGUIN

GALAPAGOS PENGUIN

There are seventeen different kinds of penguins. The smallest is the little blue penguin. It is about one foot (30 centimeters) tall. The biggest of all penguins is the emperor penguin, standing almost four feet (120 centimeters) tall.

All penguins have black or bluish-gray backs and white bellies. The patterns around their necks and heads are what make them look different. Some have colorful patches. Others show off brightly colored crests. But they all have the same basic body shape and characteristics.

All penguins are found in the Southern Hemisphere.

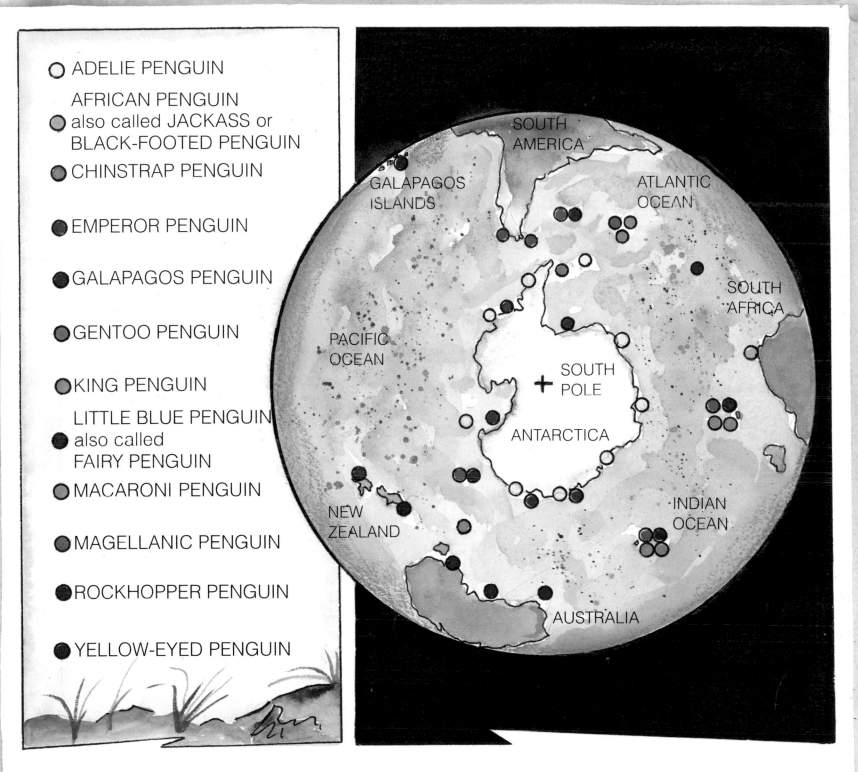

ADELIE PENGUIN

AFRICAN PENGUIN
also called JACKASS or
BLACK-FOOTED PENGUIN

CHINSTRAP PENGUIN

EMPEROR PENGUIN

GALAPAGOS PENGUIN

GENTOO PENGUIN

KING PENGUIN

LITTLE BLUE PENGUIN
also called
FAIRY PENGUIN

MACARONI PENGUIN

MAGELLANIC PENGUIN

ROCKHOPPER PENGUIN

YELLOW-EYED PENGUIN

SOUTH AMERICA

GALAPAGOS ISLANDS

ATLANTIC OCEAN

SOUTH AFRICA

PACIFIC OCEAN

SOUTH POLE

ANTARCTICA

INDIAN OCEAN

NEW ZEALAND

AUSTRALIA

The Adelie and emperor penguins never leave Antarctica.
Others live in New Zealand, Australia, South Africa, South
America, and the Galapagos and many other islands.

Penguins are birds, but they lost their ability to fly millions of years ago. Over time they began to spend a lot of time hunting for food in frigid waters. Their wings changed into powerful, rigid flippers for swimming.

Penguins have sleek, smooth bodies that glide easily through the water. They are excellent swimmers and divers. Larger ones can swim faster than 25 miles (40 kilometers) an hour. The emperor penguin can dive deeper than any other bird, about 1500 feet (450 meters).

KRILL is a small shrimplike creature.

FUR SEAL

SEA LION

SHARK

LEOPARD SEAL

KILLER WHALE

Groups of penguins may stay at sea for weeks at a time. They leap in graceful arcs through the water to grab breaths of air. Penguins feed underwater on krill, fish and other sea creatures. Their natural enemies are fur and leopard seals, sea lions, sharks and killer whales.

When the penguins want to leave the water, they can leap up as much as six feet (1.8 meters) onto a rocky shore or iceberg. They climb rocks easily, hopping from one to the other. Sometimes penguins speed over snow and ice by dropping onto their bellies and sliding!

A penguin's many feathers are small and stiff. They form a warm and waterproof covering. In really cold places, penguins have an extra layer of long, downy feathers underneath. They also have thick layers of fat to keep them warm.

Once a year many penguins come together to form colonies called rookeries. It is time for the penguins to mate and raise their young. At this time, they make loud croaking and trumpeting sounds. Most of the time penguins are quiet.

MALE

FEMALE

What a noisy place a rookery is with all the harsh penguin calls. There can be hundreds, sometimes thousands, of penguins in a rookery. They have no trouble finding their mates.

While courting, they chase each other. Sometimes they hold their wings away from their bodies and hold their beaks up high. Usually the same pair mates and raises its young together.

ADELIE PENGUIN

KING PENGUIN

EMPEROR PENGUIN

It is time to build their nests. Some penguins make their nests in burrows or rocky crevices. Others build nests in the open using sticks and grasses. Some arrange small stones in a circle. The two biggest penguins, the emperor penguin and the king penguin, don't build nests.

Soon after the nest is built it is egg-laying time. Most penguins usually lay two eggs. While one parent keeps the eggs warm, incubating them, the other one searches for food. Incubation can last 30 to 60 days depending on the kind of penguin. The penguins fiercely guard the eggs and their nesting territory.

EMPEROR PENGUINS

EGG

BROOD POUCH

King penguins and emperor penguins lay only one egg. The female quickly passes her egg over to the male. He carries the egg on top of his feet. The egg is kept warm by a flap on his belly called the brood pouch. He carefully waddles around short distances without dropping the egg. During incubation time, the female swims out to sea to feed.

The male emperor penguins gather together in the cold, dark polar winter. The temperature can get as low as –60 degrees Fahrenheit (–51 degrees Celsius). They protect themselves by huddling close together, constantly moving from the inside to the outside of the group and back to the inside to stay warm. During this time they don't eat. They fast, living off stored body fat, and can lose up to 45 percent of their body weight.

CHICK

After about 65 days the egg hatches. The female returns around this time. It is her turn to care for the chick. She tucks it under her brood pouch to keep it warm. Then the male emperor penguin is free to swim out to sea to feed.

The chick weighs about 11 ounces (308 grams) and is covered in gray, soft down. The mother has food in her belly. When the chick is hungry, the mother throws up, or regurgitates, a meal for it.

When the father returns, both parents take turns feeding and keeping the chick warm. The chick grows. When it's about eight weeks old, it weighs around four pounds (1.8 kilograms). Now the chick is too big to stay under its parents' brood pouches.

CRÈCHE

The chicks begin to gather into groups called crèches. They huddle together to stay warm. When the sun shines they scurry around getting stronger and practicing their balance.

When a parent returns, it calls with a cry only its chick knows. The chick rushes to its parent. Mealtime! The chick is fed one huge meal every few days. It takes time for the parents to make each trip out to sea for food.

FLEDGLINGS

All penguins are raised in similar ways. When the chicks are three to ten months old, they begin to lose their gray down and grow adult feathers. Now they are called fledglings.

Off they go to live on their own. They learn to hunt and survive without the help of their parents. In about four years they
will return to raise their own young.

At one time the number of penguins was declining. Eggs were harvested, and penguins were hunted for their skins. Their fat was boiled down to make oil.

Today penguins are in danger. Sometime oil spills coat their feathers. Over-fishing reduces their food supply. They get tangled in fishing nets. Tourists can do harm to colonies of penguins by disturbing them.

Now there are laws to help protect them. People work together to help penguins survive in our modern world. Some areas have been named penguin sanctuaries.

Penguins can be found in zoos and aquariums. People working there care for the penguins in a clean, safe environment.

It is fun to watch penguins play.

PENGUINS! PENGUINS!

The first penguins lived about 40 million years ago. Prehistoric penguins stood about six feet (180 centimeters) tall.

The largest penguin is the emperor. It can weigh about 90 pounds (40 kilograms).

King penguins can live to be 20 years old.

The smallest penguin is the little blue or fairy penguin. It weighs about three pounds (1.3 kilograms).

There are seventeen kinds of penguins. The five not illustrated earlier in the book are: the erect-crested penguin, the royal penguin, the Fiordland penguin, the snares-crested penguin, and the Peruvian penguin.

SNARES-CRESTED PENGUIN
(New Zealand)

ERECT-CRESTED PENGUIN
(New Zealand)

ROYAL PENGUIN
(South of Australia)

FIORDLAND PENGUIN
(New Zealand)

PERUVIAN PENGUIN
(Peru and Ecuador)